A Journey of Hope

Una Jornada de Esperanza

To Hope the sea turtle, in her journey.
May your life be long and full of adventures.
And may all of your hatchlings make it to the sea.
Thank you for being a part of our adventures.

This edition is published by special arrangement with Beautiful America
Publishing Company.

Grateful acknowledgment is made to Beautiful America Publishing Company
for permission to reprint *A Journey of Hope/Una Jornada de Esperanza*, text
and photographs by Bob Harvey and Diane Kelsay Harvey, illustrated by
Carol Johnson. Copyright 1991 by Little America Publishing Co.

Printed in the United States of America

ISBN 0-15-302199-3

2 3 4 5 6 7 8 9 10 011 97 96 95 94 93

HARCOURT BRACE & COMPANY

Orlando Atlanta Austin Boston San Francisco Chicago Dallas New York
Toronto London

A JOURNEY OF HOPE
UNA JORNADA DE ESPERANZA

Text and Photographs by
Bob Harvey and Diane Kelsay Harvey

Illustrations by Carol Johnson

Hope was late. And this was not good.

Most of her 106 brothers and sisters had gone already in the night. And now it was morning, not a good time for a newly hatched sea turtle to begin her journey to the sea.

Se le había hecho tarde a Esperanza. Esto no era bueno.

La mayoría de sus 106 hermanos y hermanas se habían ido en la noche. Ahora era de mañana, que no era buena hora para una tortuga de mar recién nacida empezar su jornada al mar.

So Hope must hurry. In the night, she had struggled free of the egg which had been her home for the last 48 days. And, together with her brothers and sisters, she had thrashed about deep in the sand, enlarging the nest cavity and moving it upwards. But, when the moment came to leave, Hope was upside down. By the time she could flip herself over, the others had gone. And now the sun was rising, a dangerous time for a young sea turtle to be on land.

Esperanza tenía que apurarse. Durante la noche había luchado para librarse del huevo que había sido su hogar durante 48 días. Junto con sus hermanos y hermanas se había revolcado en la arena haciendo el nido más grande y moviéndose hacia arriba. Pero cuando llegó el momento de salir estaba boca arriba. Cuando por fin se pudo enderezar, los demás se habían ido. Ahora el sol estaba saliendo, lo cual era una hora peligrosa para que una pequeña tortuga de mar aún estuviera en la playa.

In the cool, damp sand Hope began to climb upward. Climbing upward through the sand, she used her flippers in a swimming motion.

En la fresca, húmeda arena, Esperanza empezó a subir. Escalando por la arena, usaba sus aletas como si estuviera nadando.

After a short time, she encountered a funnel-shaped path, up through the sand to the surface. This was the path her brothers and sisters had made as they left the nest.

This was the route she too would take to the surface. Ahead, she saw light, for the first time in her life.

Poco tiempo después, se encontraba en un camino en forma de embudo que la llevaría a la superficie. Este fué el camino que habían usado sus hermanos y hermanas cuando salieron del nido.

Esta era la ruta que ella tomaría a la superficie también. Más adelante podía ver la luz por primera vez en su vida.

The sand was dryer here, at the surface. And it wanted to slide. Hope almost made it to the top of the funnel, when it collapsed and she went sliding back down.

Soon, however, she pushed over the rim. She was tired from her climb, so she paused for a moment.

La arena estaba más seca y resbalosa en la superficie. Esperanza casi había llegado hasta arriba cuando el embudo de arena se deshizo y ella resbaló hasta abajo.

Pronto se empujó hasta la orilla del embudo. Estaba cansada de escalar, asi que descansó un momento.

Here, before her, was her first look at the world. The golden sand of Escobilla Beach stretched out of sight in both directions.

Aquí, adelante de ella, estaba su primera vista del mundo. La arena dorada de la Playa de Escobilla se extendía en ambas direcciones.

Behind Hope the sandy beach blended into a heavy growth of trees and shrubs. Vultures waited here, hungrily, for the chance to eat a young turtle.

Atrás de Esperanza la playa se convertía en árboles y arbustos. Los buitres esperaban, hambrientos, una oportunidad para comerse una tortuga jóven.

Ahead, huge waves rolled and crashed into the sand. The sunlight caught the tops of the waves, making a brilliant reflection. Hope saw the reflection and knew the way to the sea.

Using her tiny flippers as legs, she pushed herself over the sand.

Adelante, las enormes olas se rompían sobre la arena. La luz del sol caía sobre las olas haciendo un reflejo brillante. Esperanza vió el reflejo y supo el camino al mar.

Usando sus pequeñas aletas como piernas, se empujó sobre la arena.

The sun was getting hot. Hope grew tired and weak. If she stopped, her black shell would absorb the sun's heat and she would die.

Slower, now, she pushed forward. A sand crab jumped out and grabbed one of her flippers. The movement of a vulture overhead frightened it away. That was close.

El calor del sol estaba cansando y debilitando a Esperanza. Si se detenía, su concha negra absorbería el calor del sol y moriría.

Más despacio, siguió empujándose. Un cangrejo saltó y le agarró una aleta. El movimiento de un buitre lo asustó. Eso estuvo cerca.

A wave rushed out over the beach toward Hope. Stopping just short of her, its foamy edge left a mark in the sand.

As Hope moved forward, the sand became wetter. The going became easier.

Una ola se acercó hacia Esperanza. Deteniéndose enfrente de ella, la orilla espumosa dejó una huella en la arena.

Mientras Esperanza seguía adelante, la arena se sentía más mojada. Su camino se hacía más fácil.

Another wave came. This one washed over Hope. It lifted her and, for a moment, it seemed it would carry her out to sea. Instead, it pushed her back up the beach a couple meters, a long way for a little turtle.

Otra ola llegó. Esta cubrió a Esperanza. La levantó y por un momento parecía que la llevaría al mar. En lugar de eso la empujó hacia la playa unos metros, lo cual era un largo camino para una tortuga pequeña.

Washed in her first bath of sea water, Hope was refreshed and full of new energy. The water had cooled her and assured her that this was where she belonged. She pushed forward.

Mojada en su primer baño de agua de mar, Esperanza estaba refrescada y llena de energía. El agua le había asegurado que allí era donde pertenecía, asi que siguió adelante.

Soon another wave picked her up. This time, her flippers knew what to do. Swimming for the first time in her life, she kept her head pointed out to sea.

Pronto otra ola la levantó. Esta vez sabía qué hacer con sus aletas. Nadando por primera vez en su vida, se dirigió hacia el mar.

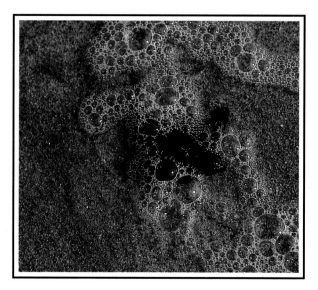

But the wave had other ideas. It pushed her far back up the beach and left her to start again. Again and again the waves pushed Hope back. Again and again she scrambled forward.

Pero la ola tenía otras ideas. La empujó hacia la playa y la dejó para que empezara de nuevo. Una y otra vez las olas empujaban a Esperanza hacia atrás. Una y otra vez seguía adelante.

Then, a wave swept over Hope from the side. Instead of pushing her back, it pulled her down toward the roar and foam. In a second, Hope was gone. Her journey to the sea was complete.

De pronto una ola llegó de lado. En lugar de empujarla hacia atrás, la jaló hacia el rugido y la espuma. En un segundo, Esperanza se había ido. Su jornada al mar se había completado.

Her journey to the sea was just the beginning of Hope's adventures. In the sea, waiting for a breakfast of young turtles, were huge numbers of large fishes and sharks. Hope must avoid these hungry enemies and hide in floating bunches of sea weed.

Su jornada al mar era únicamente el principio de las aventuras de Esperanza. En el mar hay un gran número de peces y tiburones esperando la llegada de tortugas pequeñas para su desayuno. Esperanza tendrá que evitar estos enemigos hambrientos y tendrá que esconderse entre las algas marinas.

For the next few years, we don't know where Hope will go, or what she will do. We do know that if she lives, when she is about nine years old she will return to Escobilla to mate in the sea and then lay her eggs on the beach. She will be much larger, maybe 45 kilograms.

Durante los próximos años, no sabemos a donde irá Esperanza o qué hará. Sabemos que si vive, cuando tenga aproximadamente nueve años, regresará a Escobilla a empollar en la playa. Será mucho más grande y pesará alrededor de 45 kilos.

When she returns she will come onto land for only the second time in her life. Her journey will most likely be at night.

Once she crawls up onto the beach in the night, Hope will dig a hole 45 to 60 centimeters deep with her back flippers. Into that hole she will lay about 120 eggs about the size of ping pong balls. Then she will cover the hole and smooth the area to hide the nest.

Buried in the sand, most of Hope's eggs will hatch in about 50 days. The hatchlings will repeat Hope's journey to the sea.

Cuando regrese estará sobre la tierra por segunda vez en su vida. Su jornada será probablemente de noche.

Una vez que se arrastre a la playa en la noche, Esperanza hará un hoyo de 45 a 60 centímetros de profundidad con sus aletas traseras. En el hoyo pondrá aproximadamente 120 huevos del tamaño de pelotas de ping pong. Después cubrirá el hoyo para esconder el nido.

Enterrado en la arena, la mayoría de los huevos de Esperanza saldrán del cascarón en unos 50 días. Las tortuguitas repetirán la jornada de Esperanza al mar.

Hope's egg laying journey will be as filled with danger as her first journey. This time, much of the danger will be from people. Turtle hunters will wait in boats. If they catch her, they will take her to be killed and made into soup and other things.

After laying her eggs, Hope will return to the sea, and the turtle hunters. Perhaps twice more Hope will brave the human threat to dig nests each season.

La jornada de Esperanza para empollar sus huevos estará llena de peligro al igual que su primera jornada. Esta vez el peligro será causado por la gente. Cazadores de tortugas esperan en botes. Si la atrapan la matarán para hacer sopa y otras cosas.

Después de poner sus huevos, Esperanza regresará al mar donde están los cazadores. Tal vez Esperanza regresará un par de veces y se enfrentará al peligro humano para hacer nidos cada temporada.

Sea turtle eggs, too, are in danger. Dogs and pigs, both brought to the area by people, try to find turtle nests. They dig and eat the eggs. Eggs they uncover but don't eat, vultures and other animals do.

And again, people are a danger. Eggs are dug for people to eat. It is against the law to eat turtle eggs, but many people eat them anyway.

Los huevos de las tortugas también están en peligro. Perros y puercos, ambos traídos a esas áreas por gente, tratan de encontrar los nidos de las tortugas. Desentierran y se comen los huevos. Los huevos que descubren pero dejan, se los comen los buitres y otros animales.

Y de nuevo la gente son un peligro. Los huevos también son desenterrados por la gente los cuales se los comen. Comer huevos de tortuga es en contra de la ley pero mucha gente se los come de todas maneras.

Hope is an Olive Ridley Sea Turtle. Escobilla Beach on the south Pacific coast of Mexico is the nesting beach for many of the Olive Ridleys. But the Olive Ridleys like all sea turtles are in trouble. The number of Olive Ridleys has gone down by 80% in the last 45 years.

So, Hope may not return. The days when her kind come to nest in groups of 40,000 may be ending.

Esperanza es una tortuga Golfina. Muchas de las tortugas Golfinas ponen sus huevos en la Playa de Escobilla en la parte sur de la costa Pacífica de México. Pero las tortugas Golfinas al igual que otras tortugas de mar están en peligro. En los últimos 45 años, ha bajado el número de tortugas Golfinas por un 80%.

Así que tal vez Esperanza no regresará. Puede ser que sea el fin de la época cuando las tortugas Golfinas lleguen a empollar en grupos de 40,000.

Some people are helping. Scientists are studying ways to increase the number of hatchlings from each nest buried in the sand. The Mexican military have been enlisted to guard the beaches from illegal turtle hunting and from egg stealing.

Algunas personas están ayudando. Científicos están estudiando maneras para aumentar el número de tortugas de cada nido enterrado en la arena. La fuerza militar mexicana ha sido enlistada para cuidar las playas de la cacería ilegal de tortugas y del robo de huevos.

Steps are being taken, but more needs to be done. Many conservation groups are working to help turtles. They all need our support. So that each summer and fall little sea turtles will climb out of their nests of sand and make the long journey to the sea. Forever.

Aunque se han tomado algunos pasos, tenemos que hacer más. Muchos grupos dedicados a la conservación están trabajando para ayudar a las tortugas. Necesitan nuestra ayuda para que cada verano y otoño pequeñas tortugas de mar puedan salir de sus nidos en la arena y hacer su larga jornada al mar. Para siempre.

About the Authors/Photographers

Diane Kelsay Harvey and Bob Harvey operate IN SYNC Productions, specializing in nature/travel photography and multi-image productions. Their philosophy in designing this series is that people are more likely to work for solutions to environmental problems when they have developed a caring interest. Having created communications projects for environmental organizations from several countries, they have concluded that creating an eco consciousness in the world's youth is one of the most important steps toward addressing global issues.

The story of Hope is true. The authors witnessed the perilous journey on Playa Escobilla in the fall of 1989 while on location for another project. The race to the sea was so dramatic that it inspired them to name the hatchling Hope and to share this story.

The authors wish to thank the people in Mexico who helped in their efforts to photograph and understand the Olive Ridley sea turtles. Particularly helpful were Ruben Mujica Velez, Primitivo Ramírez Silva, and Benito Hernandez Solis. The authors are most grateful to Ana Laura Tello, for her Spanish translation.

Rivendell Nature Series

By telling the story of Hope's journey, this book teaches readers and listeners about early sea turtle life and about the dangers that sea turtles face in their environment and from humans. Readers learn natural history, geography, language, cultural and environmental lessons.

Books in this series are reviewed by educators from the Rivendell School, a noted private non-profit primary education group. Each book in the Rivendell Nature Series must meet the criteria of providing learning opportunities in the field of natural resources while engaging young readers in a compelling story.

The Rivendell educators have prepared learning activities related to sea turtles for individuals and school groups. For a list of materials, please write:

Hope, The Sea Turtle
Rivendell School
301 East Stuart Street
Fort Collins, CO 80525